THE ILLUSTRATED HISTORY OF

THORNYCROFT

TRUCKS AND BUSES

THE ILLUSTRATED HISTORY OF

THORNYCROFT

TRUCKS AND BUSES

NICK BALDWIN

A **FOULIS** Motoring Book

First published 1989
© Nick Baldwin 1989

Published by:
Haynes Publishing Group
Sparkford, Nr. Yeovil, Somerset. BA22 7JJ. England

Haynes Publications Inc.
861 Lawrence Drive, Newbury Park, California
91320 USA

British Library Cataloguing in Publication Data
Baldwin, Nick
    The illustrated history of Thornycroft trucks &
buses.
    1. Thornycroft vehicles to 1988
    I. Title
    629.2'24

ISBN 0-85429-707-3

Library of Congress Catalog Card Number
88-82692

Editor: Judith St. Clair-Pedroza
Page Layout: Phil Lyons
Printed in England by:
J.H. Haynes & Co. Ltd.

INTRODUCTION ——————
—————— & ACKNOWLEDGEMENTS

Amongst the first of Britain's heavy vehicle makers, and with a history spanning at least eighty years, Thornycroft makes an intriguing subject. Its vehicles always seemed to play second fiddle to the more glamorous warships for which John I Thornycroft became famous. Yet the commercial vehicle business kept Thornycroft up amongst the top half dozen manufacturers for much of its existence, and even when its traditional road haulage market was lost it remained on a par with Scammell, or even Kenworth for export "specials". The fact that the shipbuilding side still exists adds credence to the view that the truck business might still be with us if it had not been sold to AEC. As it was its future seemed assured, yet within a year the arrival of Leyland and Scammell in the same group made Thornycroft superfluous. However, the Basingstoke factory had helped to create one specialist market which is still served by Thornycroft's famous old model name of Nubian. One wonders whether the contract to replace all those old Mighty Antar tank transporters would have gone to Scammell if Thornycroft had still been around. As it is, its large factory still makes motor components and the statue being cast in the Chiswick workshop when the first steam van was built still stands in Westminster – one cannot help but feel that the Thornycroft name is going to be around for a very long time.

If this book helps to keep Thornycroft and its splendid products fresh in the memory of readers then I shall be delighted. Thanks for this are largely due to the various people who had the foresight to preserve the historic photographs on which the book is based. Chief amongst these is my late colleague Prince Marshall and his many friends and contemporaries like Michael Sedgwick, who were preserving commercial vehicle records and artefacts long before it became a "respectable" pastime. Into this category comes Chris Taylor, who helped greatly with his knowledge of Thornycroft buses and Phil Reed at Cummins Engines, who was kind enough to pass on out-of-date photographs to me.

My thanks also to everyone who took photographs of Thornycrofts in more recent years, including Malcolm Dungworth, who actually had the pleasure (mixed!) of running some of the last regular haulage models in the 1960s. As usual the Commercial Vehicle Road Transport Club has been a mine of useful contacts (Secretary Steve Wimbush, 8 Tachbrook Road, Uxbridge, Middlesex, UB8 2QS), as has been the British Motor Industry Heritage Trust at Studley Castle, Studley, Warwickshire, B80 7AJ, where numerous Thornycroft and other car and commercial vehicle manufacturing records are maintained. Chassis numbering records are held at the National Motor Museum, Beaulieu, Hants, which show that more than 60,000 Thornycrofts were built in total – an impressive figure by any standards.

Below: Following the successful testing of the first van the small Homefield works was established for the Thornycroft Steam Wagon Company Ltd in Hogarth Lane, Chiswick near the original company's Thameside boatyard. In 1898 demand was outstripping Chiswick and a new factory was commissioned in Basingstoke. In that same year an experimental articulated four ton steam lorry was built, which was the first of this layout in Britain and probably preceded only by some passenger carrying artics in France.

Left: John Isaac Thornycroft was born in Rome in 1843, the son of sculptors Mary and Thomas Thornycroft. Brought up in Chiswick, he attended Glasgow University and in 1862 built the first of many small steam craft on the Thames, followed by the boats for Thomas Cook's Nile tours.

In 1895 his son, John Edward Thornycroft, persuaded him (John Isaac) to build a van using steam launch components. They were assisted by sons-in-law Bertie Niblett and Fred Strikland and used Thomas Thornycroft's studio for their project. The legs of Boadicea's horse, which awaited casting for a bronze still in Parliament Square, got in the way and had to be removed temporarily. The No. 1 Steam Van, which still exists and is in the British Commercial Vehicle Museum at Leyland (along with a Thornycroft paraffin engined tractor) had front-wheel drive and rear-wheel steering.

Thornycroft supplied steam vehicles for service with the British Army in South Africa at the time of the Boer War. An American sales and manufacturing company was formed in 1901 when the British firm became John I. Thornycroft & Co Ltd (and absorbed its Steam Wagon subsidiary three years later). In 1902 Thornycroft sold its first double deck steam bus for London service. Early customers included Fuller's Chiswick brewery and various London boroughs for municipal duties. An early assortment is shown here and overleaf, including a back to front steamer that took part in the War Office Trials of 1901.

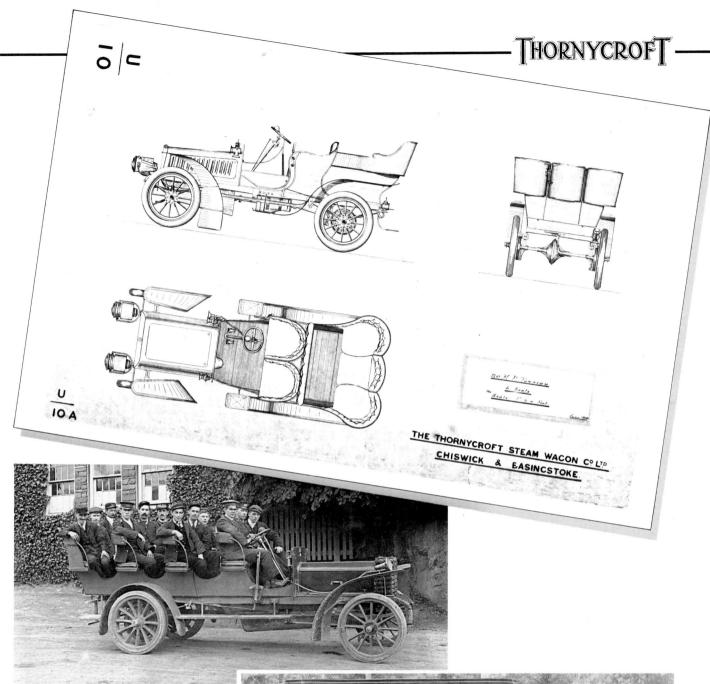

Thornycroft did not go through a steam phase with the cars it introduced in 1903. They started as 10hp twin cylinder and 20hp four-cylinder internal combustion engined cars with the modern feature of shaft drive, but the more archaic use of atmospheric inlet valves and gilled tube radiators. A 1904 20hp type is shown as well as some original plans of 1903. The little charabanc was in use in the Lake District from 1904.

Right: In 1902 the first internal combustion engined four ton "lurry" was built, followed by a 30cwt type fuelled by paraffin or petrol; the engines from these were also offered for marine purposes. The boat building side, which moved to Southampton in 1904 though Chiswick was retained until after the Great War, accounted for over 300 craft and $1^{1}/_{2}$ million horsepower of steam and internal combustion units by 1910. The "Light Van" shown was equipped with vacuum cleaning equipment in the days before more portable "Hoovers".

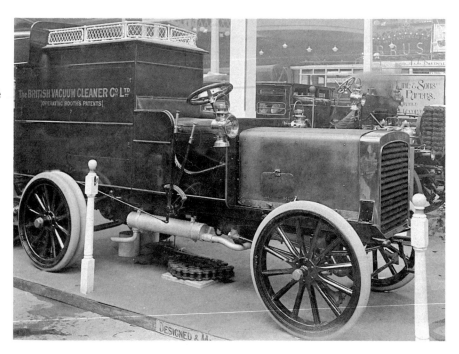

Below and opposite: In 1901 a Thornycroft steam van had become the first vehicle in the world to be equipped with radio (by Marconi). Once internal combustion had proved to be satisfactory steam was discontinued by Thornycroft in 1907. John I Thornycroft had been Chairman of the Scottish engineering firm of William Beardmore from 1901 to 1907 and a subsidiary company organised by Beardmore was Stewart and Co of Glasgow, which built Thornycroft steamers under licence from about 1902 to 1910. Here we see genuine Thornycrofts belonging to Whiteley (the 1903 London May Day Parade prizewinner is shown) and Farmiloe and also one of the last Stewart-Thornycrofts of 1910, a four tonner with 30bhp compound engine.

2633-3

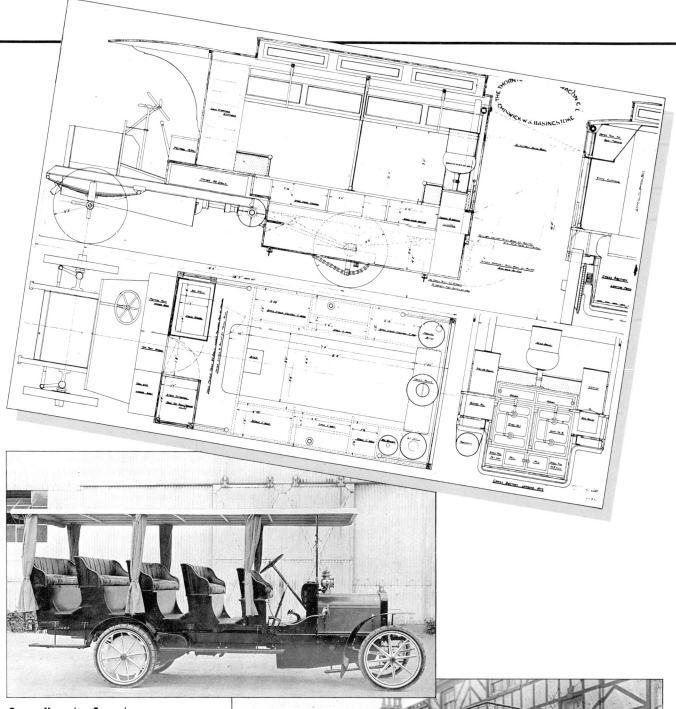

As well as its American company, which built vehicles for a few years at the Cooke Locomotive works in Paterson NJ, Thornycroft sold licences to FLAG of Genoa and Schwartzkopff of Berlin.

Meanwhile in England petrol vehicles came in many shapes and sizes including these double-decker buses of 1906, the charabanc and 16hp goods chassis of similar vintage and the "Caravan Restaurant" of 1904 shown from its plans.

THORNYCROFT 16 H.P., 2-CYLINDER VEHICLES, TYPES R & S
(as described opposite).

Thornycroft 16 H.P., 2-cylinder
25 cwt. Lorry.

Thornycroft 16 H.P., 2-cylinder
24 cwt. Box Van.

Thornycroft 16 H.P., 2-cylinder
15 cwt. Box Van. Price (without
lettering) £415.

Thornycroft Special Colonial Model "M."

SUITABLE FOR LOADS UP TO 2½ TONS GROSS ON THE CHASSIS.

This is offered to meet the large and increasing demand from the British Colonies and abroad generally, for a very strong and reliable Petrol Lorry or Van for service in localities where the roads are bad and where standard models designed for service on good roads are unsuitable.

We have specially designed this Vehicle for its work, and have made use of our large experience of service conditions abroad gained from the running of Thornycroft Vehicles and from our Colonial and Foreign Representatives.

We are convinced that a vehicle to carry a medium load not exceeding 2½ tons (2500 kilos.) gross on the chassis is more suitable for bad and soft roads than heavier types carrying greater loads.

THORNYCROFT SPECIAL 30-H.P. 2-TON LORRY, SUPPLIED TO JAPANESE WAR OFFICE.

FRONT VIEW OF 30-H.P. THORNYCROFT COLONIAL TYPE "M" CHASSIS SHOWING TIPPING FRONT AXLE.

FRONT AXLE.—A "tipping" front axle with transverse spring is provided to avoid the racking and twisting of the frame when the vehicle is traversing deep ruts or uneven ground.

SPRINGS.—Of adequate strength and flexibility. Substantial spring fixings to axles are fitted in such a manner that no holes are drilled through the springs to weaken them. For exceptionally rough ground auxiliary bumping springs can be fitted if desired.

SPUDS.—Arrangements can be made where required, BUT AT AN EXTRA CHARGE, for the fitting of road stropes over the rubber tyres of the wheels. This enables a grip equivalent to a steel stroped wheel to be obtained when traversing soft ground or wet grass, on which the rubber tyres would slip. These road stropes can only be used on soft ground and not on a hard road.

SIDE VIEW OF 30-H.P. THORNYCROFT COLONIAL TYPE "M" CHASSIS.

ONE OF SEVEN SPECIAL THORNYCROFT WAGONS SUPPLIED TO THE SOUTHERN NIGERIA GOVERNMENT

From the earliest years of the company exports had played an important part. Its 1899 steamers in South Africa have already been mentioned (though not the fact that Lord Kitchener said "The Thornycrofts are the Best)", but in 1901 a fleet of sugar cane wagons was working in Mauritius followed by steam and petrol vehicles in many parts of the world. Special Colonial models were built and in 1911 the Japanese War Office bought some of those 2¹/2 tonners with centrally sprung front axles for off-road use. Shown is an impressive fleet of charabancs in India and a page from a Colonial catalogue.

After 1904 Thornycroft cars were modernised with honeycomb radiators. They also had mechanically operated valves and came in various sizes over the years, from 14hp fours to a 45hp six. Latterly, only an 18hp model was built and it too was discontinued in 1913 to leave maximum room for commercial vehicle production. Shown here are an 18hp coupe and a 30hp laundaulette. In 1908 "JI's" son Tom entered a team in the TT and finished fifth at an average speed of 44.1mph. More successful was a Thornycroft torpedo boat which, in 1907, broke the world record at 35.67 knots.

1319-4

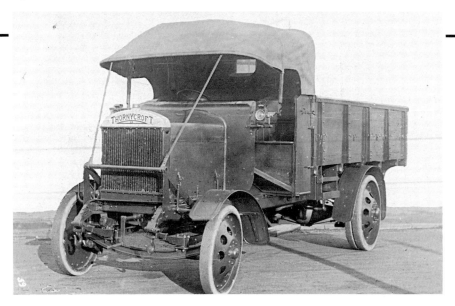

In view of its military and naval connections it was not surprising that Thornycroft was one of the first firms to offer a three tonner for the War Office Subvention Scheme. Under this civilian operators were paid to keep their vehicles in readiness for possible call-up. The first Subvention vehicle to be bought under this scheme was a Thornycroft in 1913 by the old established Pickfords haulage and storage business. With the coming of the Great War in 1914, total Thornycroft vehicle production had reached 1,360, of which perhaps a quarter had been cars. 5,000 Subvention, or Subsidy Thornycroft J types, were built in the Great War, of which two typical examples are shown here along with the highly polished 40hp engine of a similar model.

The Broken Road and lorry.

THORNYCROFT

The Heat at Dera-Ismail-Khan 1917

Thorneycrofts and 2 M T Sergeants

revious page, below left and below. More Thornycrofts in military service, this time two and three tonners aving a difficult time in India. Meanwhile back in Blighty profits, which had been running at about £50,000 er year at Thornycroft, leapt to £267,000 in 1915 and the Basingstoke factory was extended many times. arly employees had included L H Pomeroy of Vauxhall and later Daimler fame, George Burle who had egun his career with another steam engineering firm, Maudslay, and had gone on to be manager at asingstoke, and Arthur Marshall Arter who went to Lacre and British Ensign before making his own Marshall Arter vehicles. Capital of the firm was increased from £350,000 to £500,000 in 1918 and then to 750,000 in the following year.

On the road to Dera Ismail Khan

Armoured cars escorting lorries through treacherous
sands in Baluchistan 1917

"JI" (by now knighted) had entrusted managing directorship of his firm to son-in-law Bertie Niblett, but the latter volunteered for army service in the Great War, though not before building five hundred J types on spec before the first official WD order arrived. During the war, Sir John E Thornycroft was MD and the workforce became thirty-five per cent female and amounted to 1,550 at the twenty-one acre Basingstoke factory in 1920 and 3,850 at Southampton. Shown is an early postwar motorcycle rally setting out from Penrith Road, Basingstoke on the John I Thornycroft Run to Harting Hill. The solitary car is a home-made Picknell.

Like its rivals, Thornycroft started peacetime production with record order books but these soon evaporated as ex-WD vehicles flooded the market and a temporary slump held back demand. Thornycroft offered $2^1/2$ to 6 tonners, all the larger ones being closely related to the J type, which remained in production as a $4^3/4$ tonner. Here we see one of the smallest models which was powered by a 30hp engine and had a three speed gearbox and worm drive. In 1921 a similar vehicle was awarded the RAC's Dewar Trophy for meritorious performance.

THORNYCROFT MOTOR BOATS

for Pleasure Cruising

Motoring on the River or Sea has joys and experiences of its own. We build all types of Launches, Cruisers, Yachts, etc., and illustrate two recent examples (above) 100 ton M.Y. "MAHCEEB" and (left) the 48 ft. Cruiser "VITA" specially built to the order of the late Claude Johnson, Esq. Our booklet 1091 describes Thornycroft Motor Boats and Marine Engines, a copy of which awaits your request

THORNYCROFT MOTOR VEHICLES

for Profitable Transport

Every business man realises the need of Efficient Transport. Many hundreds of progressive firms are to-day relying upon, and profiting by the regular use of, Thornycroft Motor Vehicles. We build all types for Passenger, Commercial or Municipal service, each the perfected result of our thirty years' experience. May we send you particulars?

JOHN I. THORNYCROFT & CO. LTD., ENGINEERS & SHIPBUILDERS
Pioneer Builders of Motor Boats and Commercial Motor Vehicles
Thornycroft House, Westminster, London, S.W. :: Works—Basingstoke, Reading, Etc.

An unusual advertisement referring to both of Thornycroft's interests. The Claude Johnson referred to was the man who had brought Rolls and Royce together in 1904. The boat side helped to keep the vehicles afloat when serious losses were made at Basingstoke in the early 1920s, though it returned to profitability in 1925.

The J type was available from ex-WD dealers in 1923 for £140 and upwards, fully reconditioned and with a six month guarantee. This figure had risen to £300 in 1925 but even so the factory found it difficult to drum up sales when a bare chassis cost £900 new. Innovations like self-loading apparatus worked off the rear half shafts failed to impress, though richer companies like brewers and refiners continued to be good customers. Here we see an assortment of J types, old and new, in service in the 1920s.

A new model after the war was the three ton capacity X type, which shared the J type's 40hp engine and was a broadly similar vehicle though a little cheaper. Note that in view of its inflammable load this 1924 example is an early user of electric lamps.

A new range of engines of 30 and 50hp was developed in 1924 which were more efficient than their predecessors and helped to revive new vehicle sales.

Forward control versions of some light prewar models had been built, though these were possibly conversions by bodybuilders. After the war Thornycroft bowed to the growing trend and came up with bus chassis that were again closely related to the famous J type. The double-deckers were not widely used in the capital, though Redline bought a pair with Strachan and Brown bodies in 1923/4. The biggest London users at the time were Cambrian with 13, Tower Carriers and Shamrock with 3 each and Redline. The other "pirates" who tried a Thornycroft only had one, and included such evocative names as Ubique, Skylark, Phoenix, Pioneer, Legion, Empress, Fleur de Lys, Olympic and Alma. Single deckers from Basingstoke were equally elusive in London. The very strange looking forward control J type is one that worked in the Sydney area, NSW, in 1924 and was supplied by Thornycroft (Australia) Ltd. The firm also had its own branches in South America, China, Egypt, New Zealand, Straits Settlement and various parts of Africa.

Thornycroft's most successful model by far in the 1920s was its little A series, conceived initially in 1923 to qualify for a new War Department Subsidy scheme under which operators of these 1¹/₂ ton capacity 25/45hp vehicles received £120, spread over three years for keeping each in readiness for call-up. The A1 1¹/₂ tonner was also offered for 2 ton loads as the A2 as well as for passenger coachwork, and was the first Thornycroft to have engine and gearbox mounted in-unit.

A small assortment, probably all A1 types, are shown here. The futuristic one has an alloy cab by Goddards of Oadby and the BP one is known to have been chassis number 13094 for the transport of 244 two gallon cans of petrol. 1,000 A types were in use by the end of 1925.

The RASC built a heavy 4 x 4 gun tractor in 1923 from captured German components and then issued a specification for the commercially built Hathi (Elephant) Mk II. Senior draughtsman Rainbow at Thornycroft converted this into a production possibility and Basingstoke ultimately built about two dozen. They used 11.2-litre six-cylinder marine engines that developed 90bhp transmitted through a dual range three-speed (sometimes four was quoted) gearbox. They could restart on a 1 in 5 hill towing five tons and had 13 ton winches. One was converted to 6 x 6.

Right and following pages: Bus and coach versions of the A1 and A2 were immensely popular; a selection depicting some of the body styles which graced them is shown here. Several have not been positively identified but amongst those that have are (A) which has a 20 seat Argonaut coach body, (B) which is a 20 seater known as the Dragon model in 1926 (a 1923 model name for a similar type had been Patrician), (C) chassis number 12384 delivered in 1926, (D) chassis A2 Long number 14659 with Don body for Blue Bus Co. of Horsham and (E) a similar chassis number 18660 with Emerald body. Some of the big fleets of A1 models in 1926 included Devon Motor Transport with 51, GWR 40, South African Railways 40, Calcutta Tramways 38, Bombay Tramways 22, Aberdeen Corp 16 and Isle of Thanet Electric Supply Co 10. A fleet belonging to Manx Motors had covered half a million trouble free miles by March 1928.

A

B

C

D

E

PAIGNTON · CHURSTON · BRIXHAM · KINGSWEAR

THE
BURTON.

UO 9641

As early as November 1923, and well before most of its rivals, Thornycroft announced three different rigid six wheelers, though few were sold before the mid-1920s. These were usually pneumatic tyre 6 x 4 machines built with rugged Colonial conditions in mind. The smaller ones were in the A series and known as A3 ($1^1/2$/$2^1/2$ ton goods models) and A4 (14/20 seaters). Then there were the XB four-cylinder and later EC six-cylinder five tonner, and the Q (replaced by the KC) $10^1/2$ tonner. Passenger types of the later 1920s included the FC forward single and HC double-deckers. A selection of the earlier Thornycroft six wheelers is shown here: the A3 with chains on its back wheels is climbing a 1 in $2^1/2$ test hill at Aldershot.

The XB with overtracks is being tested for Shell Mex before being sent to Sarawak; the A3 with twin tyres on the driving wheels is for India; the logging A3 has an Eagle bolster; the LMS lorry is a Q model and the National Benzole tanker is an A3.

This bus is probably an A4; the
South African view dates from 1928
and shows an assortment of six
wheelers outside Borlow's Motor
Co. premises in Durban.

The part bus, part lorry
belonging to South African railways
is shown in 1931, when the SAR
fleet of Thornycrofts stood at about
150 vehicles.

From 1927 a 60-70bhp six-cylinder engine was offered in the mid-weight passenger chassis, an unusual feature being its six separate cylinders (probably similar to the later familiar idea of wet liners) which were pressed into the block casting for easy replacement and lack of distortion. The resulting 20 seaters were A6 models, sometimes known as Lightnings, with four wheel servo brakes and are represented here by an April 1928 Lightning advertisement and the canvas roof Beadle bodied example, chassis no. 16428. Those on the following pages are four-cylinder types, the two-tone bus parked by a gas lamp is the first LB (drop frame, chassis number 12927) and has a Vickers body, whilst the Haunchwood Collieries bus is a high frame Boadicea of early 1926. The others, including the BBC van on a PSV chassis, have not been positively identified. The Boadicea was no doubt named after the statue being sculpted when the first steam van was built.

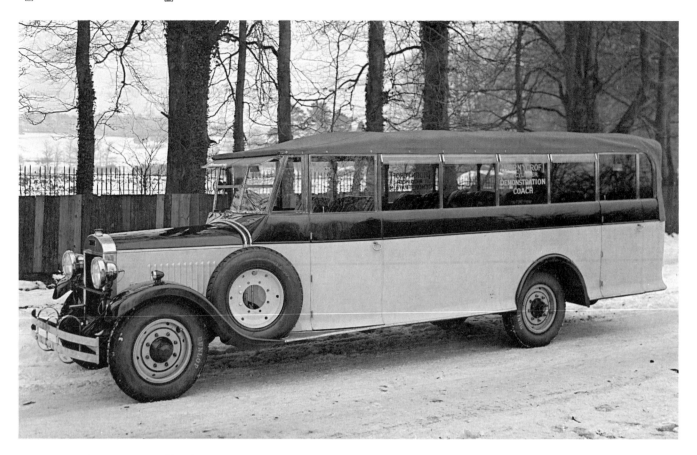

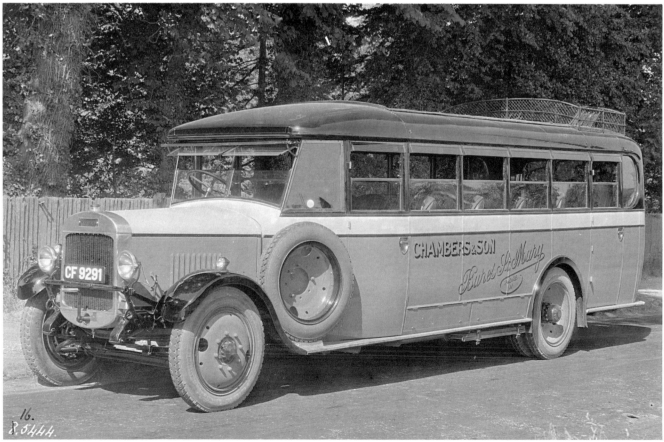

16.
8.5444.

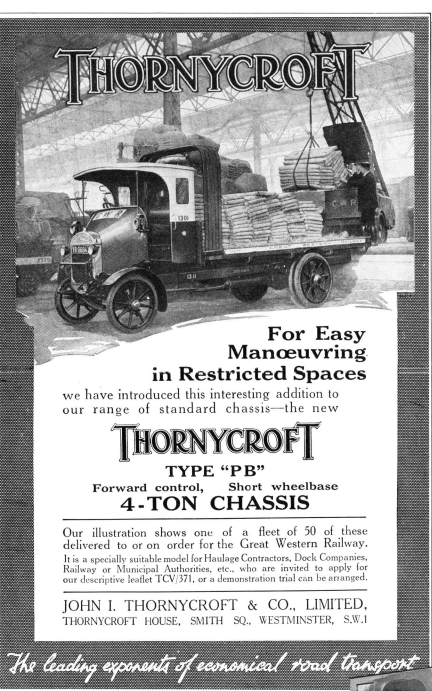

A new version of the elderly J type
arrived in 1927, known as the JJ for
five ton loads. HO6123 is an earlier
forward control version of the J,
though a very similar looking CC
model for seven ton loads
appeared in 1928. It shared a 50hp
engine with the JJ. Also shown here
is a March 1927 advertisement for a
smaller PB forward control type.
Another new contemporary model
was the KB in 1926 for three ton
loads with 30hp 5420cc four engine.

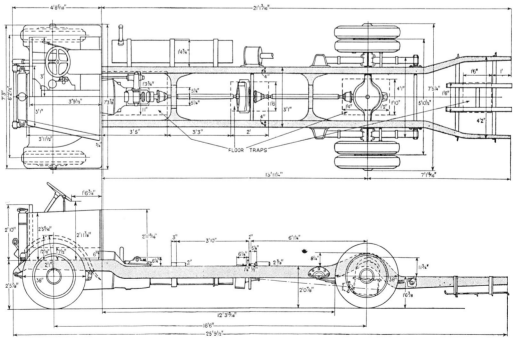

Coachbuilders' drawing of the BC Forward ZB/6 Thornycroft chassis showing principal dimensions.

THORNYCROFT

The BC Forward 32 seater (also available as a double-decker) was introduced late in 1927 and initially had a rather high and set-back driving position, as shown in the chassis photograph. From March 1929 the driver sat eight inches lower, as on the chassis depicted in the dimensional drawings. The BC had a six-cylinder 6.9-litre engine developing up to 85bhp, a four speed crash gearbox with twin plate dry clutch and underslung worm back axle. The three Bournemouth examples outside the Works date from 1930 and UE 7509 from 1928. The origins of the other two are uncertain though PG 7831, with the rounded style of radiator briefly adopted by Thorneycroft, dates from 1930 and is seen here in later life.

A fascinating bird's eye view inside the factory complex at Basingstoke in the mid to late 1920s. Note the chassis with a temporary seat for test purposes in the foreground beyond some chassis frames waiting to go to the assembly shop. The other photo of a vehicle on test shows a double-decker chassis in 1930. Sir John I Thornycroft, who died at the age of 85 in 1928, after being granted more than fifty patents connected with land and water transport. He had been chairman of the company he founded for many years, having left day-to-day running at Basingstoke to his youngest son Tom, who resigned in 1934. The eldest son, Sir John Thornycroft, was chairman and managing director.

In 1929 Thornycroft offered two types of heavy six wheel bus chassis. The FC was for single deck bodywork and the HC for double. Both had 6.9-litre six-cylinder petrol engines rated at 40.8 RAC hp, but had different gear ratios. Both rear axles were driven and vacuum servo brakes worked on the rear wheels only. KD 6499 was tried by Liverpool in 1929 and after seven thousand successful miles in the hands of an assortment of drivers, more were ordered. The one being tilt tested has Strachan and Brown

40 seat bodywork, as does the posed clerestory roof FC, which may be the same vehicle and is known to be chassis number 16350. Few of the double-deckers were sold, though Southampton had a fleet with English Electric bodywork. The later and predominantly pale one shown had Strachans (Acton) Ltd aluminium panelled 68 seater coachwork. The Brush trolleybus version was not a commercial success. The advertisement overleaf dates from 1931 when an example was tried by Nottingham.

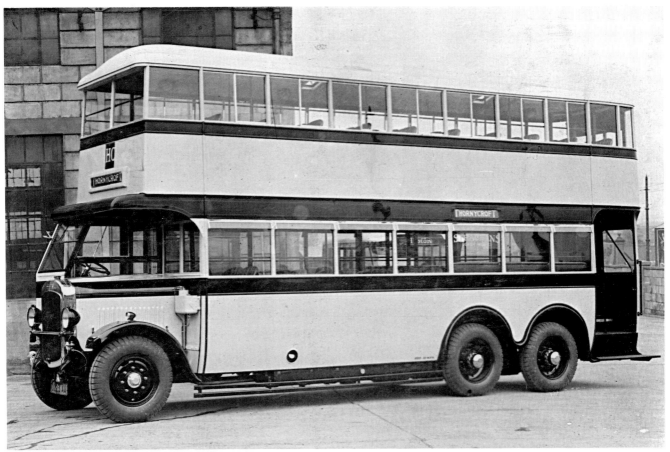

BRUSH — THORNYCROFT TROLLEY OMNIBUS

ADVANTAGES

1. Patented Thornycroft rear suspension giving even transmission of power.
2. Drive by single lightweight motor.
3. Simple foot operated control gear.
4. Powerful braking rheostatic-air-hand.
5. Comfortable well built body.

Write for New Booklet just published.

THE BRUSH
ELECTRICAL ENGINEERING Co Ltd

FALCON WORKS LOUGHBOROUGH

For a manufacturer of its size and importance, Thornycroft's sales efforts with double-deckers were abysmal: only about thirty of its LC, BC and XC models were sold in the four years to 1932. Quite why this should have been is hard to explain, though virtually everyone but the competitively priced, mass produced offerings of AEC and Leyland, were also fairing badly. One of the earliest with traditional radiator is shown here along with Strachans and Metropolitan Cammell bodied demonstrators, the latter having ''Private'' on its destination blind. The Giza bus, overleaf, started life as a Cowieson

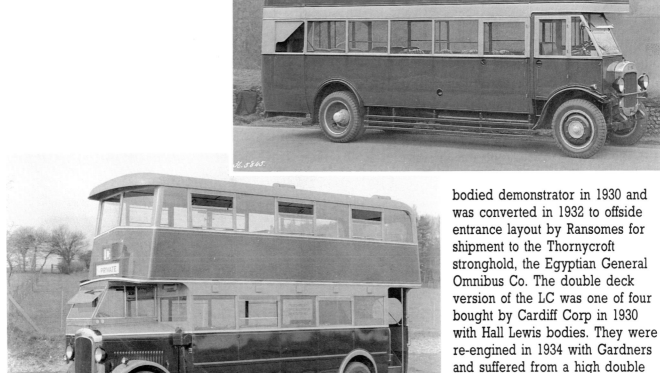

bodied demonstrator in 1930 and was converted in 1932 to offside entrance layout by Ransomes for shipment to the Thornycroft stronghold, the Egyptian General Omnibus Co. The double deck version of the LC was one of four bought by Cardiff Corp in 1930 with Hall Lewis bodies. They were re-engined in 1934 with Gardners and suffered from a high double step and bad brakes.

The Great Depression was a very difficult time for Thornycroft though it had greater reserves than some of its rivals. Amongst its advantages was, of course, its boatyards where, incidentally, the 1932 water speed record breaker Miss England II was built. The Company made losses every year between 1932 and 1936.

In 1931 the boat engine side helped Basingstoke develop a direct injection overhead valve, 10.75-litre 100bhp, six-cylinder diesel which was first fitted to a six wheel lorry but required considerable development. Thornycroft's marine engine side acquired the works of the former HE car firm at Caversham at the time and an improved 7.88-litre six was offered from October 1933. Whilst orders were few and far between there was at least a small amount of repeat business from big Thornycroft fleets like Venture Ltd, and a growing requirement for spares as operators were forced to keep older vehicles running.

In 1931 Thornycroft had an over-ambitious range of forty different vehicles, of which about half were specifically for goods. These ranged from $1^1/_2$ tons to 12 tons capacity and shown here is one of the smaller models, probably a 2 ton A10, now called the Bulldog, fitted with Eagle compression refuse body and a QC maximum weight six wheeler with six-cylinder 54.1 RAC hp petrol engine. The six wheelers were briefly known under the model name Colossus.

MOTOR TRANSPORT

The THORNYCROFT "JUPITER" will carry a full legal pay load of 6½ tons!

(Subject to type of body fitted.)

Recently subjected to a severe independent test by "Modern Transport," one of these vehicles completed the whole journey without calling for adverse criticism of any kind." Let us send you further particulars.

JOHN I. THORNYCROFT & CO., LIMITED,
THORNYCROFT HOUSE, SMITH SQUARE, WESTMINSTER, S.W.1.

ALL BRITISH CAPITAL MATERIALS & LABOUR

At the 1931 Commercial Motor Show Thornycroft adopted the "snouted" look to gain improved weight distribution and manoeuvrability. The 1932 advertisement shows a Jupiter and overleaf the 1933 ad a similar but lighter-built Taurus. Most, if not all, model names were borrowed from battleships built by Thornycroft at Southampton.

Some Definite Advantages
of the
THORNYCROFT
Snouted Type
6½-TON "TAURUS"

UNLADEN WEIGHT UNDER 5 tons with a general utility body. Tax only £43. IF (?) the Salter proposals are enforced the tax would be increased to £73 instead of £108 for most other vehicles of similar carrying capacity.

6½-TON PAY LOADS can be carried legally.

SHORTER WHEELBASE than that for the equivalent forward-control type. Enables the load to be better supported, gives smaller turning circle and better manœuvring ability.

ENGINE ACCESSIBILITY greatly increased, enabling maintenance jobs to be carried out with the greatest ease and facilitating those regular attentions which on inaccessible engines are more often neglected.

DRIVING CONDITIONS better than on forward-control vehicles. No heat or fumes.

BETTER STEERING with more rake, bringing the wheel into a more comfortable position.

BODY SPACE equal to that of the equivalent forward-control chassis.

Supplied with Standard or Long Wheelbase and Petrol or Compression Ignition Engine.

Particulars from :

JOHN I. THORNYCROFT & CO., LIMITED, Thornycroft House, Smith Sq., London, S.W.1.

and—it's BRITISH Capital, Labour and Materials.

A recent delivery to the repeat order of Messrs. Melias, Ltd.

The successful A series carried on into the early 1930s and shown here and overleaf is an assortment of goods and passenger types. The 1932/3 600 gallon tanker weighed under 2¹/₂ tons for taxation purposes. Both buses are probably 1931 models, as is the unusual artic. Quite what the Kardov van is based on is not clear; it is registered in 1933 which may make it one of the last PC 4 tonners, or conceivably a 2¹/₂ ton A7/14. These were succeeded by the 2 ton Bulldog, 3 ton Speedy and 4 ton Sturdy.

New in late 1931 was the Cygnet single decker and Daring double-decker. The Cygnet was technically a DC Forward and could also be had with normal control as the ED Charger. All, to begin with, had six-cylinder 7.72-litre 100bhp petrol engines (with a 7.88 diesel option in late 1933 and four-cylinders in some later Cygnets) with four speed in-unit gearboxes and new semi-floating rear axles. Only 14 Cygnets found customers in 1932. They subsequently sold in small numbers to various operators and there was even an order for 10 from Hong Kong in 1934 and about 50 more followed to there and Kowloon up to the end of the model in 1940. By then about 160 had been built, including one Brush equipped trolleybus for Bournemouth. After the war 5 more similar vehicles were built, but this effectively marked the end of Thornycroft as a bus maker. Shown is a 1931 Cygnet with Harrington 30 seat body that appeared at the Olympia Show in the livery of Andrew Harper of Peebles, and was actually sold to Caledonian in 1932. The 1933 plans show how 32 seats could be accommodated on the same chassis.

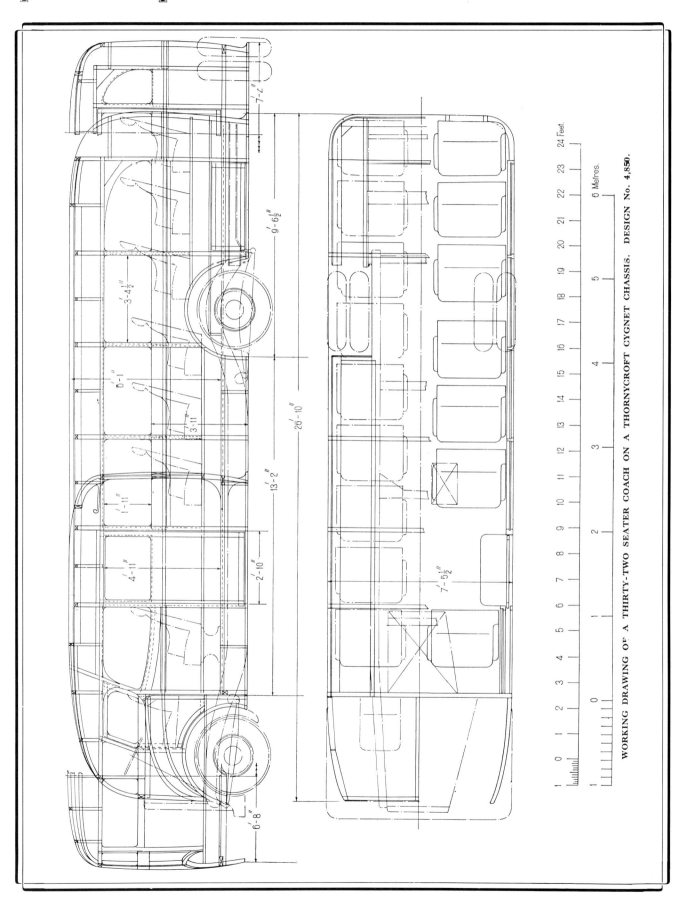

WORKING DRAWING OF A THIRTY-TWO SEATER COACH ON A THORNYCROFT CYGNET CHASSIS. DESIGN No. 4,850.

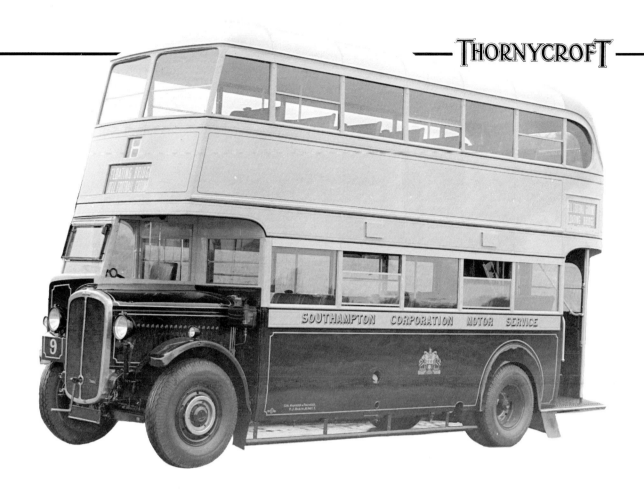

The Daring, or DD Forward, had a similar mechanical specification to the CD and ED and the new Thornycroft ribbon radiator styling. It got off to a very slow start with 5 sales in 1932 to Dundee Corp and 2 to Thornycroft's old friends at Southampton Corp. A prototype was tried with Gardner 6LW engine and sold to SHMD Joint Board (Stalybridge, Hyde, Mossley and Dukinfield). This undertaking was run by a former Thornycroft employee and was one of the few outposts where Thornycroft heavy buses were much in evidence, though often with Gardner engines. A few Darings were sold in Scotland, some with Beardmore engines, and Southampton's Darings had risen to 5 in 1934 and ultimately to 9. Shown is one of their 1933 intake with 56 seat Park Royal body. The advertisement overleaf dates from March 1932, and the dignitaries (right) are standing in front of the Giza BC already shown with one of the four original Darings on the left. It appeared at Olympia in 1931 with Ransomes body and was sold to Safety Coach Services in 1934. In all, only 43 Darings were built, plus 2 similar machines after the Second World War.

Introducing the NEW THORNYCROFT PASSENGER CHASSIS

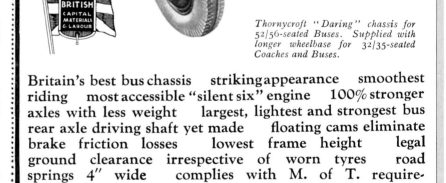

Thornycroft "Daring" chassis for 52/56-seated Buses. Supplied with longer wheelbase for 32/35-seated Coaches and Buses.

Britain's best bus chassis   striking appearance   smoothest riding   most accessible "silent six" engine   100% stronger axles with less weight   largest, lightest and strongest bus rear axle driving shaft yet made   floating cams eliminate brake friction losses   lowest frame height   legal ground clearance irrespective of worn tyres   road springs 4" wide   complies with M. of T. requirements with 56-seated body of reasonable weight.

By June 1931 the Egyptian General Omnibus Co had 108 Thornycroft buses in service in Cairo. Two are shown in a typically leafy Hampshire setting prior to despatch. Thornycroft was doing remarkably well in several export territories and in 1930 had 42 vehicles in service in Ceylon and a fleet of 100 five tonners with bus bodies at work in Bombay. The Egyptian General Omnibus Co added another eleven A12 fourteen seaters in 1932. In addition, substantial orders from Hong Kong and Kowloon were mentioned in the Cygnet caption. However, as the world recession bit so exports suffered and, taking 1929 Thornycroft sales as 100 per cent, they fell to 78, 57 and 17 per cent in the following three years.

These three highly dissimilar vehicles are badged Speedy; a model name that became widespread in 1933 on various A7 and A14 models. The bus is a 20 passenger A14, whilst the rigid lorry is an A7 three tonner with the style of radiator only gradually ousted by the ribbon type of late 1931 that appears on the 1934 artic with Eagle trailer. The A7 had a 41bhp four-cylinder engine whilst the A14 had a 51bhp six. Artic versions of the Speedy were sometimes known as the Steadfast and could have Dorman diesel engines.

Late in 1933 a new 82bhp four-cylinder diesel, initially for the 7 ton Taurus, joined its revised six-cylinder sister. Despite this, Gardner, Beardmore and Dorman diesels were also available in Thornycrofts. Lower in the weight range came the new Handy 2 tonner with 3.62-litre four-cylinder 40bhp petrol engine. It weighed only 1 ton 17 cwt as a chassis/cab and cost £340. The cab and radiator shell could be lifted off with a crane in a matter of minutes and the chassis had a turning circle of only 36 feet. The GWR and LNER promptly ordered 84 and 31 respectively and they became popular in all sorts of local delivery and collection roles. The model letter for the Handy was BE, which marked the end of the A series. A 3 ton version which followed in 1935 was called the Dandy.

In late 1933 also the Metropolitan Supply Co ordered 40 of a new lightweight six wheel model called the Stag, which was claimed to be particularly suitable for fast cruising on arterial roads. Known as the XE type, the Stag 10/12 tonner used a 100bhp six-cylinder petrol engine. It could have a Maybach preselective gearbox or Thornycroft eight speed sliding mesh unit and was said to be made from ultra-strong lightweight steel. An additional weight saving feature was its trailing rear axle.

This 1937 example is shown working for contractor John Mowlem during the Second World War.

There was an important new model at the 1934 Scottish Motor Show in the shape of the Trusty 7^1/$_2$-8 tonner with six-cylinder 100bhp Thornycroft diesel. It had the set back axle arrangement also seen on some of the bonneted models – a 1937 example appears here along with a 1935 model in service with Triplex Foundry.

Less significant at the show was the Dorman engined 3 ton Bullfinch, which took the place of the rarely seen original Tartar and 4 ton Beauty, not to be confused with the subsequent Beautyride, which was for 26 seat coachwork. Other light passenger types that succeeded the well-known A series were the Dainty 20/24 seater and Ardent 26 seater, though none sold well in view of competition from the Dennis Ace, and dominance of Bedford.

An important newcomer at the end of 1935 was the Sturdy which
weighed under three tons and could carry five tons. It had a new
four-cylinder 60bhp 3.865-litre petrol engine (above) and in-unit four
speed gearbox with worm driven fully floating rear axle. Widespread
use was made of high tensile steel and Elektron metal. On the following
pages are various forward and normal control versions of the Sturdy in
the late 1930s. The Sturdy models were in the ZE and YE series. As
artics they were rated for 13 tons gross or up to 22 tons as drawbar
tractors overseas.

P.1274.

E FRUIT & POTATO MERCHANT.

A heavy duty 6 x 4 was sold as the Dreadnought, but the first time that the familiar Amazon name appears to have been used was for this off-road 26 seat desert coach for Iraq in 1937. It had a Gardner 6LW engine, two ratio four speed gearbox and trunnion mounted rear bogie that allowed nine inches of articulation. The little forward control 20 seater of 1939 is based on the Nippy 3 tonner which had replaced the Dandy in 1937.

When war came in 1939 Thornycroft had been gearing up for military production for some time. Having completed an order for 122 Sturdy-based searchlight generator trucks they were awarded an order for 400 more. Running the sales side since 1937 had been J James, who had formerly been sales manager at Armstrong-Saurer and before that had worked for Commer from 1913 to 1927. Chief designer was Charles Burton, who had held the same position at Gilford (and before that had been with Coulthard, Rolls-Royce, Vulcan, Karrier and Tilling-Stevens), whilst the newly appointed works manager responsible for Basingstoke was R F Newman. Shown below is an appropriately liveried Hillman Minx service car and, overleaf, views of the factory contrasting 1898 with forty years later.

The last commercial motor show in London for many years was held in 1937. Here we see the Thornycroft exhibition including the Iraqi Amazon bus (the model was normally rated for $6^1/2$ tons of goods). The other bus is the new Beautyride 26 seater with Grose bodywork and four-cylinder 60bhp petrol engine. Most of the remaining vehicles are Sturdy models, including a bonneted type in the foreground. Next to it is a Trusty diesel carrying an assortment of engines.

Thornycroft became one of the most important suppliers of vehicles, ships and engineering equipment during the Second World War. At Basingstoke the 4 x 4 Nubian 3 tonner had been developed in 1938 and over 5,000 were subsequently built. A convoy is shown making a beach landing – they could climb 1 in 2 hills and travel at up to 40mph. The six wheeler is one of several thousand 6 x 4 Tartars supplied with petrol and diesel engines. This one has a workshop body but numerous other sorts were fitted.

No less than 8,230 Bren Gun and similar Carriers were supplied, plus 1,850 sets of inflatable flotation equipment for them. They were a standardised design also built by Aveling-Barford, Ford, Sentinel and Wolseley and were powered by Ford V8 85bhp petrol engines. Other Thornycroft Basingstoke products included 11,000 connecting rods for the engines of tank landing craft, 670 sets of two pounder guns and 1,700 sets of seventeen pounders. There were also 15,000 sets of torpedo rudders.

Several examples of an interesting 8 x 8 amphibian called the Terrapin were also built by Thornycroft with twin Ford V8 engines. These were conceived by Morris-Commercial and the larger Mk II version from Basingstoke is shown.

Special Thornycroft crane carriers had been built since 1935 when a batch of 12 ton 6 x 4s with Ransomes and Rapier 6 ton cranes was built for the GWR. The Amazon was widely used as the basis for the Coles EMA MK VII 6 ton crane and over 2,000 were built – a view of Amazon chassis being assembled in the works is shown. The generator to power the crane's electric controls and motors was driven from the PTO of the 100bhp Amazon. The two strangely bonneted four wheelers are Sturdy models with generators mounted ahead of the engine. They were used as water storage tenders, searchlight lorries and general purpose generators and more than 1,500 were built, taking Thornycroft's military wheeled vehicle output to 13,000 during the war, plus 2,000 civilian vehicles.

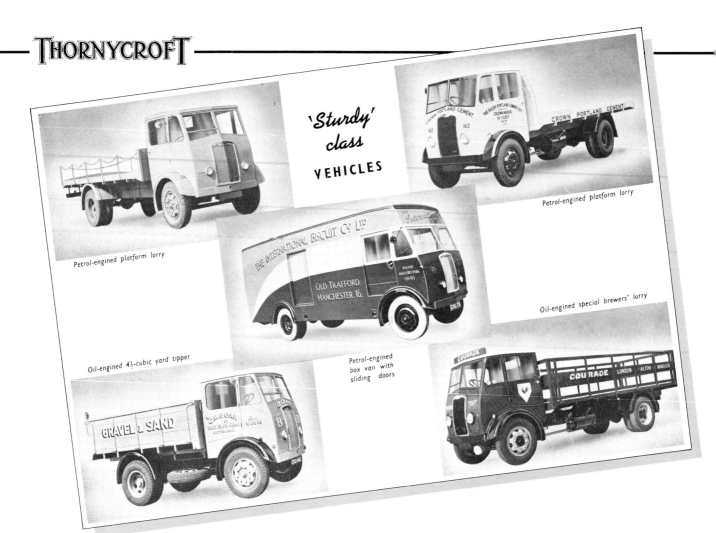

'Sturdy' class VEHICLES

Petrol-engined platform lorry

Petrol-engined platform lorry

Oil-engined special brewers' lorry

Oil-engined 4½-cubic yard tipper

Petrol-engined box van with sliding doors

A diesel (or oil, as Thornycroft called it) version of the Sturdy which had been intended in 1939, had war not intervened, appeared with indirect injection in 1944. Here are some examples of petrol and diesel versions shown in a mid 1940s service manual – which cost 42/- (£2.10) – from Basingstoke at the time. An ER4 petrol engine and its layout in the chassis from the same manual is also shown. Overleaf is the new TR6 diesel. These engines produced 65 and 67bhp respectively, the former from 3865cc and the latter from 4042cc.

An uprated version of the Sturdy, called the Sturdy Star, arrived in 1948 with a direct injection version of the diesel engine. Also new in 1948 was the bonneted Trident and a change of name of the vehicle company to Transport Equipment (Thornycroft) Ltd, a subsidiary of J I Thornycroft and Co Ltd. The reason for this was that the vehicle and ship sides were still partly under government control and were answerable, confusingly, to separate ministries.

FIG. A1. Front left-hand view of engine/gearbox unit

1. Fan.
2. Grease nipple
3. Water pump
4. Engine oil filler
5. Cooling water outlet
6. Valve tappet cover
7. Ignition coil
8. Sparking plug
9. Cylinder head
10. Distributor
11. Carburettor
12. Change speed lever
13. Inlet manifold
14. " Autovac " suction pipe connection
15. Exhaust manifold
16. Change speed selector housing
17. Gearbox oil filler
18. Engine rear support bracket
19. Engine front support bracket

20. Dog for hand starting
21. Belt adjustment groove
22. Chaincase cover
23. Driving pulley
24. Chaincase
25. Breather pipe
26. Engine monobloc
27. Dynamo
28. Dynamo support bracket
29. Oil pressure relief valve
30. Oil pressure gauge pipe connector
31. Sump
32. Dipstick
33. Locking screw, rear camshaft bearing
34. Gearbox drain plug
35. Blank flange (power take-off)
36. Gearbox casing
37. Gearbox companion flange

The Mighty Antar of 1949 onwards was originally developed by chief engineer Charles Burton for the Iraq Petroleum Co. It was intended for 32 tons GVW operation or up to 100 tons GTW, and originally worked on the Kirkuk to Banias 560 mile oil pipeline. Each pipe was 93 feet long, weighed $6^3/4$ tons and one and a half million ton miles had to be accomplished each month in desert temperatures of 20°F of frost to plus 120°F. Power came from a Rover Meteorite V8 fuel-injected 18-litre engine developing 250bhp, which was fed through a four speed constant mesh gearbox and three ratio auxiliary box to double reduction rear axles (a 4 x 2 version was also briefly offered). There were side-by-side radiators at the front holding a total of 24 gallons. Shown above is an early Iraq example on test, overleaf, chassis diagrams of the same vehicle and a pair of later examples working on the Snowy Mountain Hydro-Electric scheme in Australia. The Mighty Antar's engine was later replaced by a Rolls-Royce unit, which was ironic in view of the Rover Meteorite's origins in the Rolls-Royce Merlin aero engine.

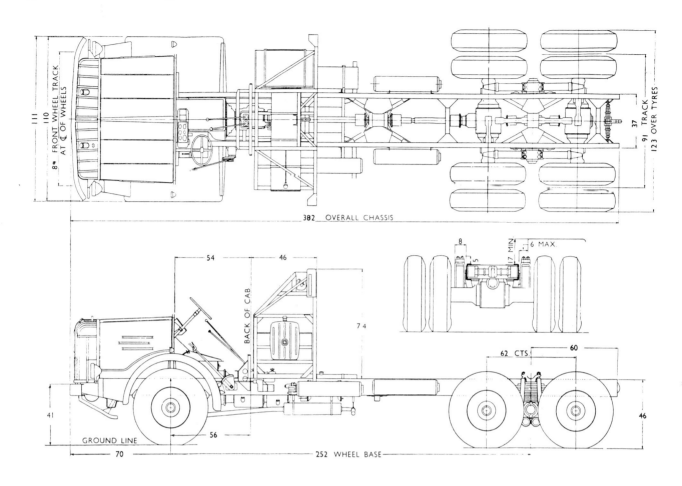

Sir John E Thornycroft KBE who, after the Second World War, was chairman for a time of the famous firm founded by his father Sir John I Thornycroft FRS LL.D (1843–1928).

Their firm continued to be profitable in the difficult postwar years, returning £128,000 net in 1945 and £144,000 in 1946, and exports boomed, including 286 vehicles for South Africa in 1948 alone.

A new face on the Board of Thornycroft was Capt. George Eyston, the holder of numerous motor speed and duration records, including an epic drive in a car powered by an AEC diesel bus engine in the early 1930s.

As well as the Sturdy and Nippy, Thornycroft, in the late 1940s, offered the Trusty with a new cab, usual NR6 100bhp diesel and two, three or four axles. Some models could alternatively have petrol injection engines. There was also the Trident in 1948 which was usually a left-hand drive bonneted lorry (though forward control was available) and had a 5.51-litre 75bhp direct injection diesel. Many of its features were also found in the Sturdy Star which entered production in 1949 but used the familiar 4.18-litre six. A few passenger chassis continued to be built, including an order for six with synchromesh pre-selective gearboxes and half cab Longwell Green coachwork for Bristol Co-op.

The well equipped factory had a rather curious assembly system whereby batches of components were sent down a track to a point where they joined the engine and other static assemblies as required. All chassis were sprayed with aluminium paint and passed through a drying oven. Gears and similar unprotected parts were covered in plastic prior to assembly or storage.

THORNYCROFT

See our latest goods chassis on

EARLS COURT
OCTOBER 1-9

STAND No. 72

An interesting summary picture of Thornycroft's 1952 Commercial Show exhibits. By then the Trident and Sturdy Star had replaced the Sturdy and used the new Motor Panels all-steel cab. The Nippy had been lightened and improved as the Nippy Star with four-cylinder petrol or six-cylinder diesel engine. The Nubian was a continuation of the famous wartime vehicle, often used as a tipper or off-road fire appliance, and could have 5.51-litre Thornycroft diesel or Rolls-Royce B80 eight-cylinder unit. As can be seen, export versions of the bonneted-type Trusty had a similar cab to the normal control Trident. 140,000lbs GTW 4x2 versions of the 250bhp Mighty Antar were very unusual and intended to compete with Euclid in the earthmover market.

FINDLATER & MACKIE of MANCHESTER LTD.

Jack Tar
Old Bonded
Jamaica Rum

A 1953 Sturdy Star 5/6 tonner with Motor Panels Mk I cab, along with a 1954 articulated version and overleaf, two examples of specialist coachwork on Sturdy and Sturdy Star chassis. The Eagle bodied refuse collector has small wheels to facilitate bin loading. The steel bodied Sturdy Star riot vehicle was one of several for Singapore in 1952 and contained radio, recording, broadcasting and filming equipment, machine gun, searchlight, tear gas and fire fighting gear. The 13'6" wheelbase version carried 32 men and the ultra-manoeuvrable 10' type 19 men. All carried wire cutters, axes and emergency equipment and were powered by diesels to minimise fire risk.

A 1955 100bhp Trusty articulated tanker shown in 1961 in company with one of BMC's new Mini vans. Castrol was an enthusiastic Thornycroft user but little by little the Basingstoke firm was losing its grip on the home market. It had placed such emphasis on exports and special overseas and off-road models that the needs of UK haulage had been somewhat neglected. The Swift and Swiftsure were new, lighter and more competitive versions of the Motor Panels cabbed mid range model from 1956. Both had new JR6 4.18-litre 80bhp Thornycroft diesels and the latter in particular achieved some success as a 30mph 6 tonner with unladen weight, even as a tipper, of under 3 tons.

The export emphasis is shown by the fact that even standard models using the Motor Panels cab (also specified by Guy) had a split waist so that the top of the cab could be removed for shipping.

The Big Ben of the mid 1950s was a close relative of the
Trusty and Nubian and was usually powered by
Thornycroft's own largest engine, an 11.3-litre unit rated
at 155bhp as a diesel and 170bhp when built as a petrol
engine. The big white dumper (above) worked in Kenya
with 11 cu. yd. rock body whilst the 1956 NCB version
has a larger capacity coal body. Overleaf, the van was
used by a British Government agency with unspecified
special equipment that included some form of winch and
hoist on the front. Normal control versions looked like
Mighty Antars and usually featured a more powerful
turbocharged version of the 11.3 diesel developing
200bhp. Examples shown are a left-hand drive chassis
and when fitted with a Motor Panels crew cab.

THORNYCROFT

BIG BEN

The Nubian was available with 4 x 4 or 6 x 6 and is shown here in tipper form for New Guinea, and as a mobile workshop with Normand bodywork for Ceylon. Engines could, as usual, be by Thornycroft or Rolls-Royce. The Thornycroft diesel of the mid to late 1950s developed a modest 90bhp, or enough for only $4^{1}/_{2}$ tons of payload on the six wheeler and rather more than 5 tons on the lighter four wheeler.

Thornycroft built a far higher proportion of the parts for its vehicles than most rivals; even the small models competing with Perkins powered rivals from Seddon and Guy had Thornycroft engines, gearboxes and axles. Higher up the weight range in 1958 came the again 95 per cent Basingstoke-made Mastiff. This was a 14 ton rigid with 109bhp six-cylinder engine and five speed gearbox. Most of Thornycroft's subsequent success with this model was, however, when it was equipped as an artic.

Thornycroft's eight wheelers may not have enjoyed as great a following as the products of AEC, Foden, Leyland or ERF, but appear to have been well liked by the operators who ran them. The only known sour note amongst this assortment was struck by the 1961 Trusty QR6 belonging to Talbot Transport which suffered from severe vibration problems leading to worn bearings and broken water and oil pumps.

Opposite & overleaf: four generations of Trusty eight wheeler are shown here, ranging from Wearing's original pattern of the early 1950s to the final versions for Talbot with the fibre-glass cab that Thornycroft ultimately used for its road-going vehicles.

CRAFT POWERED by RTR 4/2 & RTR 4/DI ENGINES

28 ft. 6 in. Fibre Glass Cruiser

24 ft. Fibre Glass Work Boat

Above, left: 14 ton Auxiliary Ketch
Below, left: Ship's Motor Lifeboat
Below: 40 ft. Twin Screw Cruiser

Marinised versions of various Thornycroft engines were built at Basingstoke and at the former HE (Herbert Engineering) car factory at Caversham, Reading. Two popular types, the 24 cylinder 350-650 shp RY12 and 2 cylinder $7^1/2$-9 shp Handybilly, wcrc produced from 1918 to 1947 and 1922 to 1955 respectively. Shown here is a fully enclosed RTR4 30bhp diesel as used by lifeboats in the mid 1950s and some craft plying with Thornycroft power in 1959. The firm also made gearing sets for other engines at the time, including AEC, Foden, Davey Paxman and Rolls-Royce. In the 1960s the basis for Thornycroft's marinising work shifted to engine components from Ford and AEC.

In the 4¹/₂ to 9 ton payload range Thornycroft still had the Swift, Swiftsure, Trident and Mastiff in the early 1960s but few were sold. The fact that they were competent vehicles is confirmed by Malcolm Dungworth, then of Talbot Transport, who remembers that the Sturdy registered 8173 W in 1960 was reliable, extremely powerful and fast when compared with rivals, had powerful brakes and was a pleasure to drive. In addition to the steel cabbed Sturdy, (below) two fibreglass cab types are shown (overleaf) plus a prototype version of the Motor Panels all steel cab that was presumably being considered at the time.

THORNYCROFT

The Mighty Antar had been a tremendous success for Thornycroft with over 750 sales by 1963. It was in use with nine armies and numerous petrol companies and civil engineers. Available with giant tyres as the Antar Sandmaster or as the R6, later versions had a 300bhp Rolls-Royce C6TFL engine driving through an eight speed Self Changing Gears compounded epicyclic box to the overhead worm double reduction rear axles.

Pictured is part of a 1963 brochure, though naturally the vehicles shown are somewhat older.

One of a number of " Mighty Antar " self-loading trucks supplied to Shell Petroleum Co. for oil-field development

Centre: A military " Mighty Antar " tractor, one of a fleet supplied to the Middle East

" Mighty Antar " tractor and semi-trailer tank transporter as supplied for military use

For
Mil
ope
—on

"Mighty Antar" tractor with 60 ton load of pipes. One of a fleet of 35 similar vehicles used in the construction of a pipe line in Iraq

Top Centre: Road train hauling a 100 ton generator; "Mighty Antars" are used in this combination by the Snowy Mountains Electricity Authority, Australia

Associated Electrical Industries Birmingham, have been supplied with a number of these "Mighty Antar" tractors for export to Argentina : they are used for transporting heavy electrical machinery

nd Civilian

ff the road

In 1960 a 4 x 4 13 ton capacity 170bhp diesel dumptruck was offered (see *Giant Dumptrucks,* another GT Foulis publication) but more successful in sales terms was the similar chassis shown here for military use. This particular type was the basis of an airportable trench digger developed by MEXE. It had a 210bhp Rolls-Royce petrol engine and a secondary hydrostatic transmission to allow it to edge forwards when digging. Other versions of the Nubian were used by the services for fire fighting, load carrying and missile handling duties.

In 1961 the vehicle bulding activities of John I Thornycroft & Co Ltd (known as Transport Equipment (Thornycroft) Ltd at Basingstoke) was acquired by AEC, which already owned Maudslay and Crossley. The Board was manned by AEC men Sir William Black, J O Bowley and J D Slater, though one director from Thornycroft days remained – R F Newman, CBE, JP, who was elected managing director. All the lighter models that competed with existing AECs were quickly discontinued and henceforth Thornycroft built only specialised trucks, of which the 6 x

6 Nubian crash tenders became the best known. An assortment (above & overleaf) equipped by different fire fighting companies, including Gloster Saro, Pyrene and Carmichael, is shown together with a chassis on test. The one for Canada was on Thornycroft's 1962 Commercial Motor Show stand. The largest had a 306bhp Cummins diesel and was introduced in 1964 as the Nubian Major, whilst the smallest gained the 124bhp AEC AV410 diesel.

THORNYCROFT

Part of a brochure for the Big Ben in 1961 showing that it resembled a scaled down Mighty Antar and used Thornycroft's own 11.3-litre diesels until these were replaced in the mid 1960s by Rolls-Royce and Cummins units The bottom right picture includes an old style bonneted Trusty in use as a mobile crane. The normal control export Trusty had by then gained the same styling as its larger sisters, as shown by the Failing equipped drilling rig belonging to Esso Standard in Libya (below).

THORNYCROFT BIG BEN

FOR SPECIALIZED WORLD TRANSPORT

Cover Picture
A "Big Ben" tractor and semi-trailer in service in a Pakistan oil-field

One of a number of "Big Ben" tractive units operated by the Qatar Petroleum Co. Ltd. It is moving a Woodfield-Ideco portable rig to a drilling site at Dukham, Qatar.

A "Big Ben" 15-cu. yd. dump truck, one of a number supplied to a repeat order of the National Coal Board, N. E. Division No. 7 (Wakefield) Area.

One of a number of "Big Ben" 6 . 4 oilfield tractors with 50,000 lb. power driven winch, and designed for "off-the-road" operation with a self-loading semi-trailer in Argentina.

A "Big Ben" road tank, operating with trailer mounted tank to carry 6,000 gallons of fuel oil to oilfield locations in North Africa.

"Big Ben" Tractor and semi-trailer in the Argentine ; Yacimientos Petroliferos Fiscales operate a fleet of these.

A "Big Ben" 6 . 4 pipe carrier being loaded by a "Trusty" 6 . 4 mobile crane; the pipes are 93ft. long.

Another variation of the "Big Ben" tractor shown here with 5th wheel attachment and ramp, ordered by Gordon Woodroffe & Co. Ltd., for Libya.

One of Thornycroft and AEC financial director Jim Slater's tasks was to mastermind the merger of major segments of the British motor industry. The takeover of AEC by Leyland took place in 1962, allegedly because Leyland was annoyed to have lost much of its South African market share to AEC companies. Slater's endeavours to interest BMC in the enlarged group failed for a time because the board of the latter company was not happy with the large number of ACV (the AEC holding company) shares held by members of the Thornycroft family as part of their payment for the Basingstoke business. In the end the differences were reconciled and in 1968 British Motor Holdings was created to control Leyland, Albion, Scammell, Rover, Alvis, Triumph, Guy, Daimler, Austin, Morris, AEC, Thornycroft and others.

AEC had initially seen Thornycroft as its special vehicle section in much the same way that Scammell had been to Leyland since 1955. Unfortunately, there was not room for two such firms, though Thornycroft managed to eke out a separate existence until 1969. Shown is a Basingstoke-built Nubian awaiting a Scammell fifth wheel coupling and Scammell Challenger semi trailer.

From 1967 the two firms were under the magagement of Frederick Clem, who was formerly manging director of Chrysler-Cummins Ltd. Jim Slater (now Sir James) went on to fame and fortune in his Slater Walker investment business. At the time of the Scammell factory's closure in 1988 the Nubian design was adopted by Unipower, so the name looks likely to pass its half century with ease.

In 1966 the original boatbuilding business of John I Thornycroft & Co Ltd merged with its rivals Vosper and Co, which had existed in Portsmouth since 1870. The resulting Vosper Thornycroft (UK) Ltd became state owned in 1977 within British Shipbuilders, but was bought out by its management in 1985 and floated on the Stock Market in 1988. It currently has a workforce of 1,900 and makes Sandown class mine hunters, hovercraft, hydrofoils and electro-hydraulic equipment.

Meanwhile, over at Basingstoke the separated vehicle manufacturer concentrated on building

gearboxes for the Leyland group as well as trailers for Scammell. In 1972 the Basingstoke factory was sold to the American transmission specialist Eaton, and Thornycroft vehicle production was transferred to Scammell at Watford. By then its principal activity was airfield crash tenders, an example of which, a Nubian major, is shown in chassis form at Watford. The completed machines have Pyrene and Gloster Saro equipment and no longer carry the famous Thornycroft "T". From 1977 the crash tenders were called either Leyland or Scammell Nubians, and in the following year were completely redesigned to accommodate rear engines, thus ended their Charles Burton design ancestry. In 1988 the rights to the Nubian and its spares were acquired by Unipower of Watford, which also assumed responsibility for Scammell Commander military vehicles. Unipower have been making 4 x 4 vehicles since 1937.

The final new Thornycroft model was the AEC 12.4-litre AV760 engined Bushtractor, developed from the AEC 690 Dumptruck, new in bonneted form in 1964. It was also built for Aveling-Barford, which had joined British Leyland in 1968, as a dumper. Production was transferred, along with the Nubian, to Scammell where it became the LD55 model. In 1977 as the Leyland or Scammell LD55 it was uprated to 24 tons gross and given the Leyland L12 202bhp diesel for use as a tractor, dumper or heavy duty load carrier. In 1973 the last of the spares and equipment were transferred from Basingstoke. Those not required, including a complete prototype fire appliance chassis intended for a lightweight Home Office order actually won by Bedford, went to local enthusiast David Hurst. Since then the old factory has concentrated on Eaton transmission components and the parts of it not converted into the Thornycroft Industrial Estate still exist in much the same exterior form as they had developed in Thornycroft's heyday as a vehicle builder.

POSTSCRIPT

As befits one of Britain's major commercial vehicle producers (its chassis numbering had reached 63500 in 1965) there are a considerable number of elderly Thornycrofts existing around the world. In Britain several dozen are actively preserved and the one shown here on a Cheshire embankment has recently been rescued from oblivion, though what became of the bus in use with a showman in the 1960s is unknown. The 1934/5 Handy is chassis BE/FB4 number 24239 and is being restored by Powell Duffryn Fuels at Portsmouth.

Many Nubians, Antars and Big Bens are still giving sterling service and are likely to be in use for many more years.